CAREER CHOICES FOR YOUR SOUL

FULFILL YOUR LIFE, NOT YOUR JOB

CAREER CHOICES FOR

YOUR SOUL

FULFILL YOUR LIFE, NOT YOUR JOB

By
Randy Bell

Published by

McKee Learning Foundation

ISBN-13:   978-0-9710549-4-3
ISBN-10:   0-9710549-4-0

Published by:
        McKee Learning Foundation

For more information, contact:

        Info@McKeeLearningFoundation.com

        www.McKeeLearningFoundation.com

TABLE OF CONTENTS

* * * * * * * * *

to
Ginny,
to
Karen

and to the many others
whose experiences motivated this writing,

and to
Joey
whose life exemplifies this writing.

* * * * * * * * *

I.

THE

CONTEXT

1. PREFACE

It is not just about discovering your career.

It is not just about finding a job.

It is all about aligning yourself to fulfill your life.

2. INTRODUCTION

Over the years and for whatever reasons, I have had many conversations with employees, coworkers, friends and family who were struggling with career and job decisions. The conversations have been either about *whether* to leave a current work situation, or *if* one leaves then whether to stay within one's chosen profession or to change career directions entirely.

These are typically very hard and slow decisions for people to make. Even when a job climate has become clearly intolerable, or one's personal goals are being severely limited, breaking a current work connection comes very slowly. In many instances, sometimes it never happens at all. Our need to hold onto what is "known," however bad it may be, often overrides what our instinct tells us is clearly a situation that needs to be changed.

There are many questions and concerns that naturally arise when looking at a career or job change. People often say they like the company, or location, or people and do not want to leave these attractions, but they do not like the particular job. Questions arise as to whether these are sufficient reasons to leave. If you do leave, will you succeed? Can you afford financially to make a change? Often unstated is the concern that "Is it my fault (or my failure) that caused this job to fail?"

In this world of options and opportunities, the question I most frequently hear is "If I want to make a change, what could I do *instead*?" And it is on that question that most people halt dead in their tracks. When one reaches a point of considering leaving a job, people most often are not looking just to do the same thing as they were doing. Nevertheless, some will ultimately default to continuing in their same role. Others will realize that making a job change concurrently provides them with an opportunity to reset their direction, their status, their way of life, their life's path. The decision to leave may actually be an easy one to reach; the decision about where to go next is typically a very difficult one and is a very slow decision process. Unfortunately, too many people ultimately reach the decision that there is no place for them to go at all, so they default to remaining where they are, or making a minor change in their circumstance, not by choice but by defeatism or passive acceptance. "This was the best that I could do" is too often the implicit message, accompanied by "it's not really that bad." Such decisions thereby lead to a limited life gone unfulfilled, with many unfortunate consequences to the individual. That sense of promise unrealized, or acceptance of a lesser opportunity, continually gnaws at the person's heart. If the person decides to make a small change, out of sync with his/her true heart's desire, inevitably that person is back to the same dilemma, the same dissatisfaction, within a short few years.

Many of these inadequate decisions result from a misdirected emphasis in people's thinking. In people's discussions about career and job changes, most of the emphasis is typically on "so what do you want to *do?*" Many people wither before that question, unable to even determine what could be options for themselves, or they feel incompetent to qualify for or obtain any other kinds of work than what they already know. So their field of options becomes very narrowly focused, or maybe never gets beyond the thinking or wishing stage.

Rather than starting out so focused on "what is the *job* I want," I believe that at these moments there are more fundamental questions really being asked of us. Each time we arrive at a job question, in fact this is a natural time in our lives when we are actually being called to really ask "Where should my *Life* be going next? What *Life* do I want to live? What are the next steps in my life's calling, or my life's purpose? Am I living in harmony with and achieving my true goals and values? How, and by how much, do I want to change the circumstances of my life, the directions it is taking, and the priorities that I need to pursue?" These are the questions that we need to address first, and then let the career or job step that we are considering flow from, and in response to, those answers.

It is to assist in answering these questions that this book is directed. It is about a way of thinking, a mindset, a view of work that should be the context for one's career path decisions. If you are secure and comfortable in the career directions you are pursuing, this book is not for you. If not, perhaps there is something worthwhile for you in these forthcoming pages.

Let us establish a few assumptions in advance:

1. You can intentionally define and live the life you look to live, if you choose to.

2. In point of fact, you have always been defining your life in one manner or another, whether passively or proactively. The subject for our

    discussion is simply what decisions will you make in the future, how will you make them, and based upon what priorities.

3. **Most all of your perceived limits are self-imposed by your own interpretations of your experiences, judgments, and expectations. To take back control over these limits and to eliminate them, you must first take personal responsibility for these limits that you have imposed upon yourself. You can no longer blame others for your limits, even where it may seem on the surface that others have caused you problems. Blaming others for your work problems serves only as an excuse for your inaction, bogs down your thinking, and delays you from making the changes you need to make.**

4. If you are clear about how you want to live your life and what your priorities and values are, the career and the job(s) you

need will be out there to support those. If you are not clear about your life intentions, you will never be clear about your job aspirations. And no job you take will sustain you for long.

5. Your life is a continual process of change. Even if you are bound and determined to keep yourself the same and unchanging, everything around you will continue its own change. So you are being changed whether you choose to admit it or not, to adapt to it or not. Your work, and your relationship to that work, needs to change accordingly over time.

6. Ultimately, the work you do, the career you pursue, the job you take, is really a <u>secondary</u> question, not a primary one. It almost doesn't matter what you *do*; it matters a great deal who you *are*.

7. Let your job <u>allow</u> you to be who you already fundamentally are. Do not let your job see to define who you are. <u>Job satisfaction will only come from life satisfaction</u>.

So let us start the real process of understanding who you are, what you are about, and how you will live in the next phase of your life, so that you can find the career or job that will allow that life to flourish.

3. AND WHAT DO YOU WANT TO BE WHEN YOU GROW UP?

The well-intentioned yet roadblock question.

The first step in this process is to understand the intensive expectations that you have been living within about your career choices. The question starts very early in one's life. *The Very Big Question.*

> *And what do you want to be when you grow up?*

A seemingly innocuous, conversational comment, often perhaps said with no real seriousness behind it. But the seed is planted: I must answer that question.

> *And what do **you** want to be when you grow up?*

And I guess I need to answer it <u>soon</u>, since everyone seems to be continually asking it of me.

> *And **what** do **you** want to be when you grow up?*

Even though I have no idea what I want to be. Or what my possibilities are. Or even if I have any possibilities. What job do I want to do for 50 years? I cannot even fathom 50 years of working.

> *And **What** do **You** want to be when you grow up?*

6

How am I supposed to know? I am only 4 years old. How do I know if I want to be an accountant, when I don't know how to count yet?

***

The pressure starts so early, so subtly, and is so constant. The choice of toys at birthdays and holidays. Doctor and nurse bags. (Do we still separate those gifts by gender?) Arts and crafts kits versus belts with plastic carpenter's tools. Enrolling in piano lessons or gymnastic lessons ("So do you want to be an ice skater [or hockey player]?") Little League ball players already with their own performance statistics and won/lost records. The pressure on achieving good school grades, else "how can you expect to be successful when you grow up?"

The child watches the parents go off to work, and how they spend their hours at home. And sometimes goes along with them on a "take your child to work" day.

Then there are parents' lives that are being relived though the child. Stage-mothers and coach-fathers guiding their child into the life that they have lived, and which must be lived yet again as part of continually holding onto or justifying their own lives to themselves. Following in Mom's or Dad's footsteps. Or alternately, guiding the child into a life different than what they have lived, the one they always wanted but never had the courage to try or the abilities with which to succeed.

"You'll be the 3rd generation in our family to go to good old State U."

"I can't wait for you to finally join the family business!"

"We always wanted a doctor in our family."

"I never went to college, but you certainly will!"

"I never had these things, but you will be successful and have all the things you will ever want."

"You need a secure degree to fall back on if you don't achieve your dreams." (Implied: you will not achieve those dreams.)

"You need a good job when you grow up in order to be happy."

"You must be successful (in your work)."

And much of all of this goes on before the child gets out of elementary school.

***

So then come the middle and high school years. The teenager is probably no more prepared then for *The Very Big Question* than when 4 years old. But s/he's been asked about it a lot more often. And been exposed to more things called "jobs." Where one may think there are now more choices, for many there is only more confusion, suffered in silence.

Some students have already begun to fail in their eyes or in the eyes of others. So a career choice is beginning to mean "now what is left over for me?" Choice is pretended through the child's perception of limited options. "What's the best job I can hope for now?"

The choice may have already been made, by the street environment or peer group within which the child lives. The gang is the family is the job, and the child is already on the job.

Or the student may still be in school, still on some seemingly positive track, still thinking that s/he has choices down the way. The standardized tests start. The series of part-time teenage jobs begins. The TV shows and the movies are now also viewed subtly but critically as introductions to what jobs are about --- cops, lawyers, forensic scientists, soldiers, spies, doctors, maybe a scientist thrown in for good measure. Movie stars, entertainers and athletes are, of course, highly visible. Computer nerds and games creators look like real fun. Chefs, artists, craftsmen seem like creative things to do; carpenters, forest rangers, adventure guides get to be outside away from confining desks. Accountants, engineers, registrars, philosophers, spiritual types, architects --- these are more difficult to get a read on; insights into these options will probably have to rely on parents, or the parents of friends, or by looking up to and respecting some adult in those jobs to confirm that these jobs are OK. Permission by association.

The college admissions people start sending out their recruiting materials. The visits to college campuses begin, perhaps first masked through sports events or science fairs, then by direct invitations to "come for a visit and meet us." Guidance counselors start mapping out college preparatory schedules and advance placement exams.

Except in a few commendable instances, most college discussion is around "job preparation." Earning a living. Ensuring that as a trained technician or college graduate you will have a job immediately when you get out of school, and job security for the rest of your life. But, first you have to decide …

"so what do you want to be when you grow up?"

The focus is clearly on you, and now you are running out of time for that decision. You have to put your answer down on The Form. The Application for Admission. Your Declaration for Life. The baseball game is waiting for you; cheerleading practice starts soon; answer the question on The Form and then you can go play. Tell me now, what do you want to be when you grow up? What do you want to do for the rest of your entire life? You have to commit to this now on The Form.

So you decide. Somewhere between panic and indifference, a decision gets made. The Answer is written down. On the Form. "There, maybe now they will leave me alone." Now I can go play ball, lead cheers, or go out on a date. Question answered for now.

***

So you've answered *The Very Big Question.* You know what you want to be when you grow up. You only have to go out and do it now.

Now that that decision is safely behind you, you can get on with this whole job or job training thing. Maybe you've picked a job that doesn't require schooling, so you can safely drop out of further schooling and go do what you now really want to do. Even learn on the job if you have to.

Perhaps you take whatever job happens to come your way at that moment; it makes the job decision easy (even if it is a passive decision), and maybe even passes the decision on to the person who is hiring you. Maybe a few months of training is required, but you can get through that for a short while and then get on with the job.

Or you go to college, which they have told you will guarantee you a good life with a good income for the rest of your life. All you have to do is pass those college courses that are in the way. But at least you now know what you want to be when you grow up. Because you are grown up! You filled out the question on The Form that shows you have answered the question. You have made your declaration to the world. Done.

Except ......

At college, there are people that you have never known before, from places you have never known about, talking about other jobs than you knew existed. You are sitting in classrooms talking about things you have never talked about before. You are listening to teachers who have done things, and learned things you never imagined before. And everyone keeps talking about how endless your possibilities are.

Do you really want new endless possibilities? You just answered that question awhile ago. Put it to bed with a stroke of a pen. Why is this question back on your table, tormenting you again?

So you must confront answering the question yet again. And you must do so quickly, because college is expensive, and time is short. You only have four years to get this all done (unless someone can keep this very large required amount of money coming in for your education). Somewhere along the line, you fill out a Declaration of Major Form, and once again announce to the world the latest version of your answer to *The Very Big Question*. Or you drop out of college to go find yourself.

If you are one of the lucky ones who is perceived as clear and knowing what you want, you may just decide to not face the question again. You answered the question once: that should be enough. You know what you want; Mom and Dad liked your answer; grades are good. Besides, promises have been made to you in return for making this decision, and you expect them to be kept. So stay the course.

Then you graduate. Or go on to graduate school, and maybe even doctoral or professional schools. With all this practice, it is easy to keep re-answering *The Very Big Question*, filling out The Form, and making continuing announcements to family and friends. If you are really lucky, you can keep this going unendingly, and never have to actually find out if your answer to "*The Very Big Question*" was a correct one.

***

Except at some point, the day of reckoning comes. Perhaps slowly; perhaps quickly. Perhaps within your first year in the workforce; perhaps in mid-life or later. Likely it comes at several points in your life.

Maybe the promised jobs do not show up after all. Perhaps each day on the job looks increasingly less than what was pictured on TV or in the movies, nothing like was described in school or by parents and family friends so many years ago. Or perhaps the people around you are impossible to deal with in their attitudes, personalities, or how they treat their work. And, of course, the boss is absolutely <u>impossible</u> and unrealistic in his/her expectations! The commute to the job, the building you work in, the time you spend in your little square cubicle (or outside in the heat, rain and snow) becomes a numbing shock to your system. It is nothing like what was envisioned. Actually *being* a fireman is nothing like you imagined when you played with the fire truck you had as a child.

Now new thoughts come up. "What was I thinking? But I have to think about the investment I have made in my job. I am not qualified to do anything else. What else can I do?"

So you change departments. Or change employers altogether, probably several times. Perhaps you go to a different city. Go from a small company to a large one (or vice versa). Start traveling in your job (or you quit traveling). Yet within a year or 3 or 5, the same kind of questions come back again, the same frustrations arise, you tell the same work stories to your family and friends. Until your really best friend finally says, "Haven't you been down this road before, with the same complaints, regardless of all the various changes you've made in the past?"

And so regardless of your age (20s, 40, 50, even in your 60s), regardless of your job, regardless of your time spent in education and training pursuits and attainments … you sit quietly in your car during commuting hours, or alone on a mountainside on a fall weekend, or in a noisy bar on an after-work evening, and ask yourself …

*And **What** do **I** want to be when I grow up?*

*****

Do I exaggerate the force, the impact of this conditioning that we experience? I do not think so. As a parent, I watched my own two children work their way through this process. One was convinced early on as a child of what she wanted to do in her life (elementary education teacher); the other created and followed his career path by responding positively to opportunities as they were represented. As a college educator and administrator, I talked with numbers of students who struggled through the Declaration of Major process, and I have followed the consistent statistics over the years about the number of changes students make in these declarations. I have listened to dinner conversations between parent and child around this work question, and watched the reaction of these children or young adults as they grapple with the answer to what they are intending to do for an education / job / career. They grapple from an ill-informed base of knowledge about the world of work, at a time when they are only beginning to even begin to understand who they are as a person, for which they feel their answer will apply to a lifetime that they can barely begin to comprehend.

I have also talked with adults at various ages and career stages who are continually coming back to the issues of career choices and job selections. Who are seeking advice and guidance for their next move in the workplace. Who are feeling various combinations of being unchallenged intellectually or emotionally or professionally, abused by the current workplace, disillusioned vis-à-vis their expectations, trapped in their current place, or increasingly disconnected from their non-work life and aspirations. In many of these instances, the person feels immediately thwarted in responding to these feelings either by seeing no options within their current career path, or not knowing what new direction(s) to pursue, or being restricted due to personal life commitments. Whether it is the first job disillusionment, the mid-life crisis, or the end-of-career setup for upcoming retirement, the question of What Do I Want To Be When I Grow Up is not just a question for the young.

This is the question with which we struggle, the question that is continually forced upon us, the question we continually seek to answer in one way or another. But it is also the <u>wrong question,</u> the one that disguises the ONE TRUE QUESTION we should be asking of ourselves. (We will come back to this One True Question later in this book.)

<u>Two overwhelming and critical observations emerge regarding this conditioning environment:</u>

- All of these forceful early discussions revolve around *what* you will do, not *who* you are about;

- There is an implicit message that there is ONE answer for you, ONE career waiting to be found and followed, which thereby ignores the reality of your multi-dimensional self.

Still not convinced of this overwhelming pressure, the importance we have made of this career decision hanging over our heads? Keep in mind that in the English language, when people began to move from a single name to adding a further identifying last name, what primarily evolved was that one's *profession* came to define who you are: Baker, Bell, Black, Carpenter, Chancellor, Cook, Cooper, Farmer, Gardner, Plumber, Smith, Steward ...

Even that most personal of things, **our name**, has been defined by the work decision.

14

Exercise: Identify the messages given to you over your life regarding careers and jobs, when and from whom. How have you responded to these over the years?

4. WHAT DRIVES US INTO A PARTICULAR JOB?

*What did **I** truly decide,*
and what did others decide for me?

We answer the Very Big Question many times in our lives. Sometimes consciously, sometimes unconsciously. Sometimes we tinker with that answer and accept a promotion or a similar job down the street. Sometimes we move out in a major change of direction and make a career change or a major geographic move.

You make your decision, because you are in charge of this answer. In charge of your life. But how did you make that decision? On what basis did you truly decide your direction? Have you really been as in charge of your life as you believe?

Many initial and often subsequent career decisions we make were in fact based upon a variety of *external* conditions, not internal.

- We responded to peer pressure, did what our friends were doing or what *they* said we <u>should</u> do.

- We moved in the direction that our parents suggested to us, whether by overt instructions or through subtle suggestions; we emulated their own careers, or we chose direct alternatives to them.

- When we found ourselves out on our own, we felt desperate to find *something, anything* to do to support ourselves. We grabbed the first available option that came to us.

- By some accident, an option presented itself to us; lacking any other apparent alternative, we chose to follow that lead.

- We took all of this education and training, and got our certifications, so then we did what was expected of us --- to actually *do* what we had learned.

- Our life situation changed (loss of spouse, supporting a family), perhaps very unexpectedly, and we needed a job --- any job --- that would support that change. We could not turn our backs on our responsibilities.

Once an initial job selection has been made, most subsequent job changes are a *re*actionary step to a currently unacceptable condition. Only infrequently are they a positive, natural, and planned progression to the next opportunity along a continuous path toward an identified target. Even when you may think they are. The drivers to change are frequently:

- You were passed over for that promotion

- You were passed over for that raise

- You were fired

- Your job, title, salary, and/or working conditions were changed

- Your job was eliminated

- Your boss was terrible, and treated you unfairly, badly, or perhaps even threateningly

- Your co-workers were not cooperative, supportive or stimulating colleagues

- The stresses were too great, and expectations of you were unrealistic

- The demands and challenges were beneath your abilities

- Your goals and energies were being thwarted

- Your ethics and character were being compromised

17

- The job sucked

Given our natural human predisposition to do nothing and stay in the status quo, it actually takes a fairly major combination or intensity of these situations to cause us to think about our job at all, much less to make any kind of change regarding it. If and when you do get around to looking at your situation, and in reaction to one or more of these types of conditions, you may either:

Chuck the whole profession, and decide to go into a wholly different, unrelated line of work. (This is the least frequent response, except perhaps during one's mid-life crisis.)

Find another job, doing pretty much what you were already doing. (A frequent and common response.) It would be nice if there was some accompanying bonus (title, position, money, or other) with that replacement job to help validate the rightness (or righteousness?) of your decision to change. Or maybe you even *require* that bonus in order to justify making the change. (Or, lacking that bonus conveniently gives you an excuse for not going through with a change).

Decide that you have no other options. (The primary response to most negative job situations.) The barriers to making a change are built upon a variety of stated reasons. You don't know what else you might want to do (what *else* you might be when you grow up); you don't know what alternative choices you might have; you don't have the skills or credentials to do something else; there are no other jobs available in this area for what you do; you are financially dependent upon this job; you are tied to this job and/or this area due to commitments to your family and/or friends. The list of reasons is inexhaustible. Whatever the selected reason(s), you grin and bear it but without much enthusiasm; or suffer under it and become bitchy and negative about most everything that arises in your job (and maybe in other parts

18

of your life). But you essentially accept it and close out other possibilities. Concurrently, quietly and almost unacknowledged, you also begin a process of steadily becoming more and more brain dead, emotionally vacant, narrowly focused, and creatively stifled.

You make a decision. But what exactly are you deciding, and how are you deciding it? If you make a change, is it based pretty much as was your original career decision? If you continue to stay put, how hard did you really challenge yourself to counter your self-imposed limitations? How easily did you simply accept these perceived limitations, and how often do you now find yourself vigorously defending the rightness of your (non-) decision against any attempt by others (or yourself) to question your reasoning?

What exactly did "you" truly decide?

Reminder: You cannot blame other people, or outside circumstances, for your current job situation and conflicts. Such an approach excuses and prevents you from moving forward with bringing your life into proper balance. The only question is, what can YOU do to make your job situation right?

---

5. WE'RE ALL TEMPORARY WORKERS

All jobs will end.

For most of the world's history, careers — if not jobs themselves — were lifetime decisions. Soldiers, farmers, homemakers, traders and artisans were roles established early on in life and continued until one could no longer work. In twentieth century Japan, jobs were a marriage contract between worker and company; commitment to company was returned as a commitment to worker through life-long employment. Lifetime job guarantees were a key objective of the mid-20th century American labor movement. For those of the generation of the 1930s Depression era, a permanent job with steady income was to be valued and held onto, not to be discarded easily. Longtime work experience was prized by employers, even if their reward structure did not always seem to fully reflect that prize. Tenure in education became institutionalized not just at the college level for recognized accomplished scholars and educators, but it also became a right for all teachers including public grade school and high school teachers, making employment termination virtually impossible. Once *The Very Big Question* was answered, the expectation was that the decision would be honored and protected by one's profession. The job would be there forever.

"Forever" is a relative concept. To the 20s-something entering the workforce, the next statistically anticipated 50+ years of life is rarely thought about. End of life cannot be seen on the horizon, except perhaps in the lives of *other* people who are in their old age. To the 70s-something, 50 years will have passed by in a blur, and end of life is seen all too clearly on the horizon.

In the second half of the twentieth century, many long-term job commitments have disappeared. In the non-competitive industries (primarily the governmental and educational workplaces), instances of long-term or lifetime employment still occur. The very stability of those environments will attract employees for whom stability is a primary job attraction. But in the competitive industry environments, responding to change is the basis for successful long-term existence, and changes in work mean changes in employment. Perhaps some will stay in their industry of choice, through a succession of employers; a lesser number will stay with their companies, but move through a series of changing jobs within; few will last their lifetime. In the former monopoly industries, where lifetime jobs used to be a natural attraction (ATT; IBM), turnover is now the norm. High technology has typically been 3-4 year jobs, depending on whether boom or bust years. In real estate, agents are often change-of-life careers, frequently changing employers every year or two.

But regardless of how long you may stay at one job, the truth is:

- your job will ultimately be eliminated (or changed beyond recognition), either by the company going out of business, downsizing, changing operations, changing missions or line of business, automating, or because you are (rightly or wrongly) deemed incompetent to perform the job; OR

- you will quit or retire

<u>So regardless of what your intentions or expectations may seem to be, your job will end.</u>

This reality of **ending** is a Fundamental Truth that you will need to accept. And this Truth leaves you with only two options:

- *Fight it*, but understand that you will unavoidably lose your true self in that fight

21

- *Accept it*, but position yourself to manage it in your favor

Most often, we take the "fight it" position, even though we rarely see it or express it in those terms. <u>We live in fear</u> of losing our jobs, rather than living in the excitement of finding our personal opportunities. We form The Compact:

> I accept this job, I will give you my time and work; you will support and insure my life's needs. And the job will go on, if not forever, at least until *I* choose to end it. It is all about MY decision. So I will make my plans accordingly: buy my home, plan my family, anticipate retirement, commit to a (usually continually growing) lifestyle. Because that is The Compact.

Yet something inside gnaws. The fear remains. The knowing at some deeper level that it will all end at some moment. And if it ends too soon, before you would choose, there is the quiet belief that you will not be prepared for the consequences. The greater this quiet internal fear, typically you give into it all the more. You cling even tighter to The Compact. You accept a worsening work environment, minimizing the significance with each event, choosing from a variety of explanatory excuses. The deepening dependency between you and your job may be obvious to others, but it is rarely obvious to you; you become comfortable in your excuses and rationale. You ignore the impact on your physical health, the impact on your relationships with others, the lessening of your self-respect, the increasing frustration at the doors being closed to you, the continual giving away of more private dreams and personal intentions, the growing mental numbness, the devaluing of your person and what you have to give. You do this because you have come to believe that this is the way a job works, the way it is supposed to be, and it's not so bad after all.

> "This work is all I can do. I do not have other choices; my circumstances do not allow me to be free to make other

22

choices. I do not challenge that, because it is pointless. I am still committed to my last iteration of the answer to the *Very Big Question.*"

But are you *really* that limited? In your skills, in your choices?

I don't think so. You have many skills, and many choices.

Can you believe in you like I believe in you?

Recommendation: Accept from the outset that your job is temporary. It will only last a finite time: days, months, perhaps some years. Probably before you are ready for it to end. But it is only <u>when</u>, not if. So <u>prepare yourself</u> to be ready when the time comes to go. And do not overstay your welcome.

---

6. IT REALLY DOESN'T MATTER *WHAT* YOU DO

The Realities of Workplace / Workforce / Education.

You know what? In the long run, it really does not matter much what specific career path you follow, what job you do. *How* you go about selecting that choice is <u>vitally</u> <u>important</u>. But let's put ourselves in a proper perspective about this whole work and job question, and the specific answer you are seeking.

In the final analysis, there are only three options that should govern any career selection:

- a job that in and of itself reflects and fulfills your life purpose

- a job that supports fulfilling your life purpose through other non-job activities

- a hybrid combination of the above brought into a proper balance

When I conduct focus group sessions or interview people, whenever possible I try to find out what someone's career path has been, their work story that has brought them to their current place. I like to ask groups "how many of you are now employed doing something that is directly related to your major in college?" Rarely do more than two hands go up out of ten responders. (This proportion changes somewhat depending upon the age distribution of the discussion group.)

Within the higher education community, the latest statistic with which I am familiar was that @<u>40</u>% of students change their selected major at least once before they graduate. Typically

24

@40% of students at 4-year institutions do not continue from their freshman into their sophomore year at the same institution[1]. (Up to 15% dropout is considered an excellent continuation; 60% dropout warrants an investigation into the institution.) For various reasons, only 67% of entering college students complete their baccalaureate degree in six years[1]. It was recently published that 39% of adults ages 25-34 have a college degree[2], and 20% of men and 26% of women over 25 have finished four years of college[3]. Working adults who are enrolling in online educational programs and courses are one of the fastest growing segments of the education market, reflecting continuing learning and credentialing but also anticipated changes of careers.

Midlife and retirement life career changes are becoming the standard, not the exception. Given our increasing longevity, the advancing of retirement ages, the greater geographical mobility of our population, the breakup of the traditional family, and changing attitudes about aging, lifelong careers followed by a gold watch retirement party are seen less frequently. Significant career changes from midlife on are very much in evidence, although age discrimination in hiring continues to be problematic. (According to one study, younger job seekers are 40% more likely to be called back for an interview than those 50 or older[4]). Expectations for careers are also being driven by more fundamental values and personal expectations: in one study, 57% of Americans 50-70 years of age say they want a job that gives them a greater sense of purpose; 50% want jobs that contribute to the greater good, now and in retirement[5]. The number of workers 55-64 will grow 51% from 2002→2012; 70% of older workers plan to work past age 65 or never retire[6].

And what about the traditional success outcomes and work effort expended? Half of Americans earn less than $30,000 per year, 70% less than $50,000, and 90% less than $100,000. The total hours worked by men and women are roughly equal — about 65 hours per week — when you count paid and unpaid work. Americans average 46.2 weeks of work per year, versus @41 weeks for major European countries. It takes a janitor an average of 103 hours to earn $1000, a farmer 57 hours, a high school teacher 43 hours, a doctor 13 hours 5 minutes, and a chief executive 2 hours / 55 minutes. Yet it takes Brad Pitt only 4 minutes and 48 seconds to earn that same $1000[3]!

Towards what end? The following story about *The Fisherman and the Investment Banker*[7] may give us pause to reflect:

The American investment banker was at the pier of a small costal Mexican village when a small boat with just one fisherman docked. Inside the small boat were several large yellow fin tuna. The American complimented the Mexican on the quality of his fish and asked how long it took to catch them.

The fisherman replied, "Only a little while."

The American then asked why didn't he stay out longer and catch more fish.

The Mexican said he had enough to support his family's immediate needs.

The American then asked, "But what do you do with the rest of your time?"

The fisherman said, "I sleep late, fish a little, play with my children, take siesta with my wife Maria, and stroll into the village each evening where I sip wine and play guitar with my amigos. I have a full and busy life."

The American scoffed. "I am an Harvard MBA and could help you. You should spend more time fishing, and with the proceeds buy a bigger boat. With the proceeds from the bigger boat you could buy several boats. Eventually you could have a fleet of fishing boats. Instead of selling your catch to a middleman, you could sell directly to the processor, eventually opening your own cannery. You would control the product, processing and distribution. You would need to leave this small coastal fishing village and move to Mexico City, then Los Angeles, and eventually to New York City where you will run your expanding enterprise."

The fisherman asked, "But how long will all of this take?"

To which the American replied, "15-20 years."

"But what then?"

The American laughed and said "That's the best part. When the time is right you would announce an IPO and sell your company stock to the public and become very rich. You would make millions."

"Millions... Then what?"

The American said, "Then you would retire. Move to a small coastal village where you would sleep late, fish a little, play with your kids, take siesta with your wife Maria, and stroll into the village each evening where you could sip wine and play your guitar with your amigos."

Is your life far ahead of you, yet potentially coming around full circle? Is your true life around the next corner, not a distant speck in your eye? Is your aspired life already here?

II.

THE

WORKING

STEPS

7. WHAT ARE YOUR PATTERNS OF CAREER/JOB HISTORY?

*Our illusions of personal control
over career decision-making.*

Exercise: Chart your work influences and history. See and examine your patterns to date.

---

1. Given all of these background considerations that we have discussed in the previous chapters, what were the environments that nurtured you and shaped your attitudes toward work?

2. What were your parents' attitudes toward life in general, and to their own life in particular?

3. What were your parents' attitudes and values toward career / job / work?

4. What were the toys given to you in your youth? Which did you spend time with, and which did you ignore?

5. What were the work exposures you had when you were young, and how did you react to those?

6. What were the conversations that you have had about careers and jobs, and with whom? Which ones made strong impressions on you, either positive or negatively?

7. What career decisions have you made thus far, and why do you think you made each of them?

8. Have your career decisions been fairly consistent and on a straight line, or widely varying with a number of significant turns?

9. Have your decisions been *reactive* to your early environment and exposures, or *consistent* with those influences?

10. Have any of your career decisions been in response to specific lifestyle or personal life changes that have occurred? What were those changes, and how did you respond to those milestones?

8. YOUR JOB STORIES

Where Have You Already Been?

Exercise: Complete the Job Inventory Analysis questionnaire below.

Job Inventory Analysis:

Answer the following questions regarding your current job and the previous four jobs you have held (either with different companies or major changes/transfers in job positions or duties within the same company). Use a separate page for each job.

1. Your job title.

2. Your starting and ending (or current) salary &/or total compensation.

3. Your length of time in the job.

4. List your duties and responsibilities.

5. Did you supervise other people?

    • If yes, how many?

    • How well did you handle this supervisory role?

    • What did you enjoy about supervising?

    • What did you not enjoy about supervising?

6. Did you have financial or budgetary responsibilities in this job?

   - How well did you handle this financial responsibility?
   - What did you enjoy about having financial responsibilities?
   - What did you not enjoy about having financial responsibilities?

7. Describe the typical work schedule and time off structure of this job.

8. How much pressure was present in this job?

9. By what criteria was your performance measured?

10. Describe your boss/supervisor regarding leadership qualities, management competency, planning skills, people skills, and personality.

11. Describe your relationship with your boss/supervisor, both personally and professionally, regarding such things as respect, trust, honesty, communication, rewards, motivation, career development, etc.

12. Describe your co-workers and your relationships with them.

13. Describe the overall atmosphere and environment of the company.

14. How effective were you in performing your job?

    - How was your effectiveness impacted by your skills and limitations?
    - How was your effectiveness impacted by the opportunities and support (or lack thereof) provided by your boss/supervisor and/or the company?

15. What did you really <u>like</u> about this job and the working environment?

16. What did you really <u>not like</u> about this job and the working environment?

17. Why did you leave this previous job (or why are you thinking about leaving your current job)?

Summary and Review:

18. How are your answers to these questions <u>similar</u> across the five jobs you have listed?

19. How are your answers to these questions <u>different</u> across the five jobs you have listed?

20. What patterns do you see emerging from this job inventory analysis?

9. WHAT ARE YOUR REAL SKILLS?

It's More Than The Box You Are Currently In.

In order to begin to more fully understand the many possibilities that can be available to you, you first have to stop seeing yourself only in your present job, your current circumstance, your current label or job title. Your current job is not all that you are. Your current work is not all that you are capable of doing. Whether it is your capacity for a greater quantity of work, or working at a greater level of challenge, or your interest in a completely different field of endeavor, you have many different options to choose from — *if* you are willing to make <u>balanced choices</u>. But you must be able to see yourself differently than the box you are now in, the presentation you currently make to the world. If you cannot see this different image of yourself, then certainly no one else will be able to, and most certainly not those people who can open the doors you will need to pass through to make your change.

Exercise: Fill out the four Inventories presented below. Preferably, work with a person who knows you well and can help you see yourself from an outside view, and can suggest things in your repertoire than you may not see so easily. Attempt to see the full range of what you have done, what you can do, what your *talents* truly are in a <u>broader</u> more <u>generalized</u> way than just the tasks that you have been doing in your recent jobs.

SKILLS INVENTORY – TASKS

Based upon the Job Inventory Analysis you completed in Chapter 8, first itemize the many skills you have accumulated by looking at the job tasks that you have performed, both in your current job as well as in your past jobs.

Complete a worksheet similar to below based upon the duties/responsibilities for each of the five jobs you listed in your Job Inventory Analysis. Use as many lines as you may need.

For example, if you list one of your Job Duty/Responsibilities below to "1. Answer customer questions," it may involve such Skills as:

a) answering phone call inquiries
b) looking up answers to questions
c) referring customers to proper offices/personnel for further servicing

Duties/Responsibilities	Skills You Performed
1.	a.
	b.
	c.
2.	a.
	b.
	c.
3.	a.
	b.
	c.
	(etc.)

SKILLS INVENTORY – CAPABILITIES

Now try to see how those detailed skills translate into a greater picture of You. Take each of the skills you listed above, and identify your greater capabilities that those skills demonstrate.

For example, if your job is to "answer customer questions on the phone," and you do it well, the assumption is that you have:

a. good people interaction skills

b. the ability to research questions and obtain answers from reference sources

c. the ability to communicate information clearly to other people

Transform your perspective of your everyday individual activities into a larger profile of your capabilities that could potentially be transferred into a variety of different work situations.

Complete a worksheet similar to below for each of the Skills You Performed listed in your Skills Inventory - Tasks above. Use as many lines as you may need.

Skills You Performed	Capabilities Evidenced
1.	a.
	b.
	c.
2.	a.
	b.
	c.
	(etc.)

SKILLS INVENTORY – INTERESTS

Now look at the skills and abilities you have learned in your non-job activities: your hobbies, entertainment, charity work, social relationships, family interactions, etc. These are also an important part of you. The first advice normally given to a would-be writer is "write about what you know." That similar advice could well be given to the job seeker. There are innumerable stories of people who have taken their hobbies, their interests, or their recreation, and have successfully made one of these their prime career objective. If insufficient talent or personal conditions does not allow for being in a forefront role, then an ancillary position may work out just fine for you. So the painter / photographer runs a framing shop to meet his/her financial needs; the quilter runs a fabric store and teaches quilting classes; the sport enthusiast that is good with math and knows all the statistics becomes the statistician for the favorite team; the vacation traveler becomes a tour guide or operates a travel agency. Each person in such a role is surrounded by the topics, conversations, and people that really excite them.

Complete a worksheet similar to below for each of the hobbies and interests that you have, and the skills and capabilities you demonstrate within each. Use as many lines as you need.

Skills You Performed	Capabilities Evidenced
1.	a.
	b.
	c.
2.	a.
	b.
	c.
	(etc.)

FINANCIAL INVENTORY

One of the most difficult hurdles that people perceive to a career change regards their financial status. The sense of current financial commitments to be met, fears of financial risks, and assumptions of minimum income expectations frequently immobilize one's desired movements. It must be understood that the more you pursue possessions, the more you value possessions as an <u>exterior</u> statement of your worth (a statement to yourself and/or to others), and the more you seek *guaranteed* financial security, you will achieve these only by paying some cost in your personal freedom and choices. Where you set your personal level of values vis-à-vis costs is your individual choice to make. There is no one formula or standard that applies to everyone. But it is crucial that you see that choice clearly and understand what price (in dollars and non-dollars) you have elected to pay for that choice.

In your career planning it is therefore required that you get a thorough understanding of your financial picture and distinguish between those expenses that are *truly required* to sustain your basic needs, and those that are *truly optional*. For example, I do not have the skills to maintain my automobile, but I do not have to have a housekeeper to clean my house no matter how nice it may be to have such a service. Any job choice you make will need to support your financial needs that are truly required; your optional expenses are your points of freedom, and will represent the life choices that you determine.

Complete a worksheet similar to below to itemize your living costs. Be sure to include not only the expenses you actually pay each month, but also the monthly average for those expenses you actually pay quarterly, semi-annually, or annually. A friend or financial advisor is often helpful in this exercise. Tracking your out-of-pocket cash expenses for one month and reviewing your credit card statements and your checkbook detail are helpful tools for this exercise. It is very important to see this inventory ***in detail*** for the exercise to be fully meaningful. Use as many lines as you need.

Type of Expense	Period*	Monthly Amount	Required or Optional
Total Expense Each Month			

*out-of-pocket, weekly, monthly, quarterly, annually, other)

Note: In conjunction with this financial inventory exercise, this may also be a good time to review your investment commitments, debt load and payments, and other financial structures to be sure you are optimizing these for your financial benefit and to have available the best flexibility for your decision-making.

10. **WHAT IS YOUR LIFE ABOUT?**

The ONE TRUE QUESTION that really matters.

Let us forget about the question of a job for a moment. Let us think about the YOU, independently of your career and job. If we eliminate the demands of your current job, the job title, the economic benefits or shortcomings, the rootings of the place in which you now live, the friends and family with whom you engage each day, and the debts and bills to be paid this week — who is this person that remains, stripped bare of all these external ornaments?

In the upside-down thinking that we have typically created, career and job have often become primary objectives unto themselves. And by making those our single-minded pursuit, the life we live tends to fall out as an after-thought of where our career has taken us. It was once said, "We work, and then we die." No, we *live*, and then we die. The job that we do is really simply to sustain our human existence, to provide one of the tools we need so that we can be about what our life *truly* is. How that job fits *into* our life (instead of vice versa) is the true career challenge that faces us.

The reality is that we have very little control over the workplace in which we toil. A bit more control, perhaps, if we are self-employed, but even then we still have limits because we are so interdependent upon so many other people and things in order to succeed in our efforts. But we can have a great deal of control (though perhaps not absolute) over how we think, how we act, and how we live. And this is the One True Question that we really need to answer first, before all of the other decisions that we make:

How Do I Want To <u>Live</u> My Life?

All other decisions are humbled to this decision. All other decisions are secondary, and should do nothing more than point to accomplishing this primary answer. It is all about your personal goals, purpose, priorities, choices, and options. It is the stuff that comes from deeply within, that reflects your unique soul.

This is not pie-in-the-sky stuff, nor touchy-feely musings. Unless you choose to make them such, in which case you are in fact using those opinions as the basis for determining and choosing your individual answers about your life. You can choose to accept external limits before you have challenged them, or you can choose to risk defining your life for yourself instead of allowing others to do so for you. Turning the job question over on its head is something you can do, a path you can follow, albeit not an easy process to pursue given all of our prior conditioning. Answering *How Do I Want To Live My Life* is all about understanding yourself, your priorities, your values. It is the Who of you. Those things should lead you to the What that engages your time and energy, not the other way around.

Exercise: Fill out the Personal Life Inventory presented below. Take your time with these questions. Once again, preferably work with a person who knows you well. That person may encourage you to see beyond your surface immediate answer, and can perhaps help you see yourself more deeply. <u>Do not base your answers on your current job or personal life limitations</u>. Attempt to see the full range of who you truly *are* (and could be), versus who you may have become at this particular time for other reasons.

PERSONAL LIFE INVENTORY

Job Considerations

1. Why do you work?

2. How important is a job or career within your overall life's activities, goals and values?

3. How important (High, Medium, Low) are the following components in your evaluation of your job satisfaction?

    ( ) Salary and income (independent of your actual financial needs)

    ( ) Specific profession or industry

    ( ) Specific job within that profession or industry

    ( ) Position Title

    ( ) Having respect and support for your job from the company

    ( ) Having respect and support for your job from your immediate boss/supervisor

    ( ) Having respect and support for your job from your co-workers

    ( ) Having respect for your job from family and friends

4. Do you prefer:

    ( ) a very structured job
        (repeating expected tasks, consistent workload)

    ( ) a very unstructured job
        (changing tasks, "peak and valley" workloads)

5. Do you prefer a very regular work schedule, or a very irregular work schedule?

6. How important for you is time *off* the job for other activities that interest you?

7. Do you like to be challenged by your job, or do you prefer to minimize pressure on yourself?

8. Do you prefer a regularly paid fixed salary each week or month, or to be paid based upon your performance?

9. In what type of setting do you want to work?
    - a large company
    - a medium-sized company
    - a small company
    - work at home
    - work for yourself

10. How important is having interactions with people as part of your job?
    - with co-workers within the company
    - with clients or customers
    - through face-to-face interactions versus by letters and emailing

10. Can you sell things?
    - products
    - services
    - ideas

11. Are you a good teacher of people, in various kinds of circumstances?

12. Are you a good:
    - writer
    - speaker
    - communicator

13. What kind of job(s) is your worst nightmare?

14. What is your ideal working situation and environment?

15. What do other people say about you and your work?

16. How do you measure your own success in your job?

Personal Considerations

17. In what type of setting do you want to live?
    - large city
    - medium-sized city
    - small town
    - isolated

18. What characteristics about that setting appeal to you?

19. Do you enjoy traveling, whether in a work function &/or for recreation and vacations?

20. Do you enjoy being indoors at a desk or outside in the field?

21. Do you primarily enjoy working with your mind or with your hands?

22. Do you enjoy:
    - designing things
    - fixing things
    - using things?

23. Do you primarily like doing one thing at a time, or doing several things at a time?

24. Do you tend to finish what you start, or get antsy to move on to other things before you are done?

25. Would you consider yourself an organized, detail-oriented person?

26. Are you a planner or more of a go-with-the-flow person?

27. Do you consider yourself a "creative / generative" person or more of an implementer?

28. How tied are you to your present location and living situation, and why?

29. How tied are you to your present financial situation, and why?

30. What changes in your present life could you make easily?

Priorities

31. If your current commitments to finances, family, job or other responsibilities did not exist, how would you be living your life?
    - what would be the same
    - what would be different

32. What are your most important personal values?

33. What are the most important things that you would like to spend your time doing?

34. How will you measure "personal success" in your <u>life</u> (versus in your job)?

As a follow-up to the Personal Inventory above, ask yourself the following question repeatedly <u>15</u> times, writing down your answers *quickly*:

QUESTION	ANSWER
What Gives Me Joy?	
What Gives Me Joy?	
What Gives Me Joy?	
What Gives Me Joy?	
What Gives Me Joy?	
What Gives Me Joy?	
What Gives Me Joy?	
What Gives Me Joy?	
What Gives Me Joy?	
What Gives Me Joy?	
What Gives Me Joy?	
What Gives Me Joy?	
What Gives Me Joy?	
What Gives Me Joy?	
What Gives Me Joy?	

All of these answers work together to help you clarify How Do I Want To Live My Life, the Life You Seek To Live. Whether for the next month, the next 5 years, or as long as you have remaining on this earth. It does not matter if this picture changes over time. It likely will. This is a this-moment-in-time understanding. And that is fine, and actually as it should be. You are not a static being; it is your obligation to continue to learn and refine your understanding of who you are, and to exploit those learnings over time as they present themselves to you. That continual growing and adjusting is a major piece of what human life is all about. Whether we like it or not, all of us change, our world changes, and we must blend these changes together as we move ahead.

11. HIRE THE EMPLOYER OR JOB THAT WILL FULFILL YOUR LIFE

Bring It All Into Balance.

If you are now clear about the life you wish to lead, and you understand the tools you have to work with to live that life, then it becomes a matter of matching the two together to make it all happen. Simple enough, huh! No, but it is simpler than we might protest it to be. The necessary parts can be brought together and stitched into a changed life, but certain things are required.

1. **Mindset**: your conviction will need to be that living your life in the manner you want it to be must be your primary driver; the job serves only to support that chosen life, not to define it.

2. **Understanding**: you will need to develop and maintain a good sense of who you are about, and how you are seeking to live.

3. **Courage**: you will need to go against many of your previously held convictions and thought processes, and you will need to push yourself through the resistances that will naturally arise.

4. **Independence**: your changes will likely challenge many others around you, including some very close to you; some of those individuals may exert significant negative pressure on you regarding what you are doing, and you must be willing to act independently of these pressures.

5. **Acceptance**: you will need to be willing to accept the life you have chosen, and give yourself permission to live it.

6. **Success**: you will need to adopt a definition of "success" that is true to accomplishing your chosen life, rather than using the success measurements of others.

7. **Commitment**: you will have to make time for this effort; you may have to go it alone in this effort, and stay with it through some rough spots.

If you have put these personal requirements into place, then you will need to develop your own individual gameplan for achieving your life's goals.

Step 1 - Scout the territory.
There are innumerable forms of work out there. The workplace, and how work is being performed, is changing rapidly. It is a world of employees and the self-employed; of workplaces and working from home; of indoors or outdoors; of resident jobs and traveling jobs; of making sales, buying things, or keeping records of those sales; of designing or building; of manufacturing or craft making; of farmers and grocers; of entertainers, chefs and waitstaffs; of travel agents and tour guides; of fundraisers and social workers; of creating computer software or using that software. The list goes on and on, of different industries, different component pieces of those industries, and different lifestyles accomplishing those pieces. You need to see how big your potential playing field is.

- Visit libraries, your local office of your state Employment Security Division, or various non-profit agencies dealing with job training to examine their reference books describing various kinds of jobs and their forecast for future workforce needs.
- List the jobs of 30 of your friends, and what they do. Talk to them about their particular job and how it works. Then have them tell you what other people in their company do.

- As you go through the day, take note of what jobs people are doing as you encounter them. Also note the services you are needing that require you to encounter them, since you have invited them into your life.

- As you get ideas of potentially interesting areas of work for you, seek out people in those fields and ask them to tell you about their work. How they got into it, what they like about it, and what they do not like. (But remember that their satisfaction factors are based upon their own life needs, not yours!). What it looks like behind the scenes. Most people will be more than happy to have this conversation with you.

- In some instances, try the possibility on for size. Offer to volunteer time, or work at a small wage, to work in some capacity in a job environment that you are interested in. It does not matter whether or not you would be doing the actual volunteer work or not for the job that you are interested in: just see the workplace site for what it is truly like on the inside, and all of the different functions that go on to make it work. Or offer to serve as an apprentice to a master in the field in exchange for the work exposure and experience. For example, if you are considering becoming a bed and breakfast owner, try helping out running a B&B for an established owner, including making the beds and cooking the breakfasts for a month's time.

- As you see all of these work opportunities, make note of their structures: when they occur during the day or throughout the year, where they occur, working conditions, financial options, etc. Review these opportunities against your various Inventories that you completed in the previous chapters. How do these opportunities match up?

- Be slow to reject opportunities that may not seem to be natural for you at first blush. The answer may not present itself to you on the first hearing; but one possibility you reject may still lead you to consider another related opportunity. For example, if being a doctor does not match up, being an EMT, a laboratory assistant, or a post-surgical therapist may be a perfect match for you.

Remember that your first instinct will be to look for a new career or job in your familiar playing field, one that resembles what you are already doing and know about. Typically if you follow that route of familiarity, what you come up with for choices will likely appear to be very limited. Resist that tendency, and play to the underdeveloped facets of your life. The true opportunities for you are probably nowhere on your radar screen when you begin this pursuit. But those are the very ones you want to find within this process.

Step 2 - Identify Choices:
Determine your options, based upon:
- what different kinds of work, career, or job would make possible the life you wish to live?

- what work would meet your needs for sustenance, as well as concurrently provide you access to the things that are really important to you?

- what jobs would provide you with some of your life goals already built in, and what jobs would serve to support your life requirements outside of the job? (Either approach is acceptable!)

Step 3 - Choose:
Make a tentative career or job choice. The career or job you want to do that will best support you and How You Want To Live Your Life.

Step 4 - Map out your Transition Plan:
Once you have made some choices about your new career opportunities, measure how far you are away from your goal. If

your needs are fairly similar to your current circumstance, the changes required may be quite minor. But if your goals are significantly removed from your current situation, then a more significant change effort will be required. And it will likely take longer to accomplish. The more significant the change, the more unlikely you will be able to accomplish it overnight. But it can happen if you are patient and deliberate in your efforts. Do not let distance from your goal discourage you; the journey to that goal is as important as the destination.

You now need to define a Transition Plan to take you from where you are to where you wish to be. The Transition Plan needs to identify what steps are needed to take you to where you are seeking to be. Your Transition Plan will likely include such things as:

- Where you will get the additional education or training needed (online courses; formal certification programs; part-time program at a college; fulltime program at a college; apprenticeship opportunities)

- How to get to where the new job may be located (if a move is required)

- How to restructure your finances to provide for either the transition requirements or for the different income the new work will provide

- Who will be the people you will need to open some doors and provide introductions

- What will be the timeline required to do each of these transition things.

Step 5 - Go or No Go:
This Transition Plan is often an early test of your true willingness to make your desired life happen. More education or new training may be required; a geographical move may be

needed; a temporary or permanent reduction in income may be necessary (and will be likely when you are changing to a new profession where you have no demonstrable experience). And here is where all of your "can't do's" will pour out amidst waves of defeatism:

- "I can't afford to do this."
- "It is too much work."
- "It will take too long."
- "My family will not support me doing this."
- "I have too many other responsibilities right now."
- "What will people say of me."
- "I can't afford to go back to school." (or "I've been out of school too long.")

As the eloquent old gentleman once said so poetically, "Horse Petunias!"

If you truly want to make the change, then these concerns are actually fairly irrelevant, no matter how real and scary they may seem to be in the moment. They are relevant only in relation to your will and commitment. Yes, you may not be able to do all that is required *right now* all at once. Your goal may necessarily be more long-term than short-term. But that is not the same as relegating it to the "wish list / wouldn't it be nice" part of your brain. <u>Long-term objectives do not happen in the future; they happen now, in partial steps that lead to that objective</u>. All of the interim decisions and actions you make are deliberate steps that move you toward that target in defined and measurable ways. As you take these steps, you are already your goal; it just has not fully matured yet.

If in fact that goal turns out to be just a wish, a pipe dream, that's OK too. It is all right to have our little pool of fantasies that go unfulfilled as long as we do not brood about or regret them. I will always think that it would be a neat thing to solitarily hike the full length of the Appalachian Trail on my own, but I do not expect it to happen. Knowing what it would take to make this hike happen, there are simply other higher priorities in my life. So my little fantasy of standing atop Mount Katahdin in Maine on a colorful October day, doing my little dance of success, will remain just that: a nice, inspiring small image in my mind that has no real substance of importance to me.

What is important with your fantasies is that you know them for what they are and acknowledge them so that they no longer distract you. It simply means that you have clarified your intention, that in fact your priorities are different. Pursuing such a choice would not bring you into the balance you seek. In these clarifying instances, you simply need to go back and review again your Personal Life Inventory, your Skill Inventories, and your selections in Step 2 above. Then see where your next choice takes you. Trial and error is certainly allowed in this process.

Step 6 – Hire Your Employer:

Once you have identified your career / job selection, go hire the job and the boss and the company you need to support yourself in this selection. Or create your own company, and be the boss to yourself that you need.

The mechanics of obtaining the job, the interview process, or starting your own company are details and issues beyond the scope of this book. There are many excellent books, resources, agencies, and personal counselors out there that can assist and guide you in this often formidable task. I defer to, and refer you to, those avenues to guide you through this step.

Our job in this writing is to ensure that your <u>mindset</u>, your <u>purpose</u>, your <u>way of thinking</u>, and your <u>mental independence</u> at this point are fully clear. This clarity is critical so that you manage your own way through this hiring process, with the understanding that it is YOU that must do the hiring ――― of the company and people you need to support your true work.

Step 7 – Or Stay Put With A New Perspective:

If you work through this discovery and decision process, and ultimately conclude that in point of fact the job you have right now is a *positive* (versus default) and *appropriate* answer to your life's needs, that is a fully acceptable outcome. If this is the case, then be satisfied with that answer, embrace it fully, and appreciate the effort you have made to arrive at that realization. Then approach your current job with a renewed appreciation for what it represents ――― warts and all. Understand that the everyday shortcomings of that job are not that important if overall it is contributing to what you have identified are your real intentions in your life. Be a positive force in bettering your situation wherever possible. If the shortcomings were really that significant, then you would have arrived at a conclusion to change. And if the shortcomings really are that significant, then go back to Section II and start your decision methodology once again.

Remember: what you are after is a career or job that will support the life you choose to live, incorporating most all of the component parts of you. There are *many* jobs that you could do, have the talent to do, and you need to affirm the fullness of the capabilities that you have. But some of those options will not accomplish the life fulfillment you are after. Several may. You may have to work through several possibilities before you find the one(s) that fits your life balance at this particular stage of your life. There is no failure in accomplishing the important realization of what does *not* work for you. They are, in fact, important lessons to learn all through life.

III.

THE

OUTCOMES -

YOUR LIFE

12. STRATEGIES TO COUNTER THE "CAN'T HAPPEN"

Make and Keep Yourself Ready.

As was mentioned before, at some point in this change planning you will inevitably come face-to-face with your fears, and the laundry list of supposed reasons why your desired change cannot happen. Typically the hurdles I hear from people who elect not to pursue their desired life center around five areas of perceived restrictions:

- financial limitations

- maintaining existing relationships

- staying in place geographically

- lack of qualifications

- networking structures

Some of these restrictions may in fact have viable reasons for concern. But most are actually merely reflections of our fears, our self-doubt, our lack of guarantees that our changes will be successful. If we choose to accede to these fears, that can be right for us; by doing so we simply acknowledge that our priorities have been reordered, and that our desired life at this moment is to live in fulfillment of these reordered priorities. What is critical, however, is that we make this a conscious and acknowledged decision of choice on our part, and not continue a lifetime of blaming "outside factors" for our decision. Taking personal responsibility for who we are, what we choose, and what we do, is an ever-present obligation we have to ourselves. We have chosen this life we have, we have not been forced into it.

If we have identified our goals and capabilities quite honestly and reasonably accurately, the truth is that we can probably accomplish whatever life we have truly determined if we are willing to take the necessary steps that that life requires. It may take time; it may take a series of successive steps to get there; it may require reordering and reprioritizing our lifestyle; it will likely require a major focus and energy on our part, rather than letting ourselves be scattered across many well-intended but distracting other activities; it may well require us to do this alone, at least at the beginning. How committed are we to achieving this life we have identified for ourselves?

To get through these fears we first have to acknowledge that that is all they are: our fears, our doubts. Fears and doubts feel real to us, but they have no substance except what we give them. We move through them not by denying them (for they will still be with us for some time along the way), but by first acknowledging them and then by just refusing to let them stop our movement. We start executing our Transition Plan from Chapter 11, taking small steps to build our confidence and to lay the necessary groundwork. We try not to reach too far too fast; we have patience, because we know this is a long-term change not a quick-fix. We break down daunting major change into small accomplishable steps that allow us to adjust and fine-tune our strategy as we need to along the way.

Where necessary, we learn to build the *capacity for change* as part of our lifelong way of living. We know that it is likely change will happen to us more than once, that we will likely have to face this prospect and this process once again down the line. So it is important to ensure that we are continually well-positioned to deal with the five hurdles to change listed above.

Financial Limitations

As far as financial limitations, we need to be prepared at any point in time to reduce our living costs so that we can take advantage of opportunity when it comes. Ideally, <u>at least</u> **30**% (preferably more) of your net income should be covering what are truly *optional* expenses. This is money you could lose tomorrow and still be able to cover your basic mandatory survival costs. This may sound like an impossible goal in your present situation, especially given the level of debt (especially that notorious credit-card debt) that is reported by most individuals. But if living your true life and having the freedom to change an undesirable life or a negative working environment are more important to you than your possessions and toys, the image and the opinions others have of you, and other's people's measures of wealth and success rather than your own, then you *can* reset your financial position to give you freedom instead of being your prison. Your salary may well be in another's hands; but your costs are in your hands.

> "And when the farmer has got his house, he may not be the richer but the poorer for it, and it be the house that has got him ... for our houses are such unwieldy property that we are often imprisoned rather than housed in them ... But I would say to my fellows, once and for all, as long as possible live free and uncommitted. It makes but little difference whether you are committed to a farm or the county jail."
> —Henry David Thoreau

Recommendation: Review your Financial Inventory completed previously. How much could you eliminate tomorrow if you had to? What steps do you need to take over time to get yourself to that "30% Optional" target?

Relationship Limitations

Losing existing personal relationships is certainly not an easy thing to do. Especially ones that are close, deeply felt, and long-term. If you have determined in your priority setting that your relationships are in fact one of your primary drivers, then your work choices will likely need to be subjugated in order to fulfill these relationships. And having done so, you will appreciate your job for allowing those priority relationships to happen.

But if other priorities have emerged for you, then it is likely these relationships will necessarily change. Whether by moving away to a new locale, or discovering that some people cannot accommodate "the new you," or the significant instance of the breakup of family or marriage, you may find yourself surrounded by new faces and new relationships. These changes may have to be one of the necessary costs of achieving your personal fulfillment. In the case of an investment banker who chose to become a minister, his wife divorced him. The explanation offered was "I married an investment banker, and that's what I want[8]." Some old relationships may have to be maintained on a more part-time basis, or from a distance. Some relationships may not be able to make the transition, if those relationships were based upon some previous point-in-time version of you. New and good relationships are in front of you and will come your way if you are open to them. Do not live in the past of your old relationships; remember them fondly but restructure or put them in the past where they now belong.

Recommendation: Meeting new people is difficult for many of us. Practice making new friends even if you currently have a full circle of friendships. Improve the manner and frequency by which you maintain your long distance friendships from the past. Whatever skill and comfort level you have in this arena, improve upon it. This will give you added confidence that you will survive if you find yourself having to give up current relationships or needing to gain new relationships.

Geography Limitations

If your life change requires a geographical change, this also can be a difficult adjustment period. The sense of "place" is similar to the sense of people relationships. It is an important tie that gives boundaries, roots, familiarity and confidence about what to expect. A Southwesterner sees multi-hued colors in the desert where a New Englander sees only browns; that same New Englander senses a warmth and protection in green forests where the Southwesterner feels claustrophobia and a yearning for the distant horizon seen far over an open space. That first night in the new house in a new locale can be a low point in your sense of loneliness. But if you have the exploring spirit of Columbus, the curiosity of the child, and you arm yourself with the address of the local tourist bureau or Chamber of Commerce, then a whole new world of discovery can await you. It is part of the joy of making your change.

If you continue to pine for the old relationships, the old lifestyle, the old surroundings, the old haunts and recreation spots, that is when you will feel lonely and tempted to return to that familiarity. As long as you continue to talk in and of the past, you will mentally remain in that past, and you will be more and more tempted to return to where you have been (even though that past likely no longer still exists as you now remember and fantasize about it). If you have made the choice for something new, then embrace it fully; do not spend time talking about your old life in your new environment. Your new life will take time to fully unfold, and it will have many moments of doubts and awkwardness. But you came to this new place for a reason. Embrace that reason and live your new life fully.

Recommendation: Travel! Make one of your lifestyle cornerstones consistently getting out of your current surroundings and visiting other places. Understand firsthand what other environments exist, what places on a map look like in real life, how other people live and what their land and climate are like. When you are there, do not fall into the "Ugly American Traveler" syndrome, always complaining about how things there are not like they are back home. Of course they are not; that's why they are somewhere else! It is not about better or worse, it is simply about different, and being open to experiencing that difference in order to learn and grow from it.

Qualifications Limitations

If qualifications (or lack thereof) is one of the hurdles you perceive, then develop a life pattern of continually keeping yourself trained and exposed to new skills. Even in your present job, the rules, tools, and the nature of how the work is performed are no doubt changing continually. One of my most painful experiences as a technology manager was interviewing job candidates who had been let go from their previous position due to their company replacing longstanding installed technologies, older technologies that these candidates had concentrated on and specialized in, thereby not keeping up with the changing tools and new opportunities of their profession. Or they had held on possessively to a narrow job role, building a little empire in which they were the "critical only one" and thereby seemingly irreplaceable. But their critical importance was also the anchor around their neck that kept them frozen into position, unable to be moved into future emerging roles, unable to be ready for the changes that would inevitably come. Many were blindsided by what was coming. When their specialty was ultimately replaced, they were now at a dead end with nowhere new to go. For many, the personal shock of no longer being irreplaceable, no longer being needed, with no preparation in place for other options, was a blow to their personal identity and self-worth that would take years to work through. In thinking that they had a strategy to protect and guarantee their life, they had in fact surrendered control of their life to others and to external movements. Keep yourself ready to move and adapt when unanticipated change is forced upon you.

Recommendation: Keep educating yourself, whether through employer-offered programs if available or on your own initiative if necessary. Keep volunteering for selected new activities when they become available. It is very hard to adopt a change momentum when you have been following a status quo inertia.

Networking Limitations

Lastly, it is important to identify early in this quest allies and personal resources that can help you through this process. Those people who will not agree with your statement of limitations, but who will encourage you to think those limitations through carefully. Who will not encourage you to jump off a cliff blindly, but who will also not inflict their own personal opinions and fears and values onto your needs. These may be people already in your inner circle, or new people that you will need to seek out, both

67

professional advisors as well as people that are involved in areas that are of interest or concern to you. If you are honest with them as to your intentions and concerns, you might be quite surprised how many people in everyday walks of life will be willing to spend some amount of time and share technical information with you. Each person you talk with, and each new piece of information you obtain, will often lead you to yet another outreach, a continuing cycle of information-gathering that you need to accomplish. So there is no reason to be embarrassed at asking your questions. Just be sure to *listen* to these people, without argument, and try to also find out what brought them to their current place and perspectives; it is all more information. You can make your own decisions later as to what is pertinent or not to your situation and directions.

Recommendation: Find yourself 2-3 close advisors that can hopefully follow you through your process of discovery and decision, and who can keep you honest. Don't be afraid to move from them if you find you start bumping up against their limitations. And most importantly, avoid the naysayers of this world.

13. **THE SPIRITUAL COMPONENT**

The Universe Factor.

There is a tendency to feel that you are all alone in your process. That the full weight of your decision, and carrying through on that decision, are solely on your shoulders. This can be quite a heavy burden to carry alone. But it does not have to be this way. You will more likely be ultimately successful if you expand your personal support network.

I have already mentioned in several of the preceding exercises to consider engaging a friend or professional advisor in some of your inventory analyses. Such individuals can help you question your own initial answers, provide other suggestions, and listen to your thought processes. Not to argue with you — in fact, avoid such arguers completely — but to help you deepen your self-evaluation and see through your own delusions, prejudices, and pre-conditioned thinking.

A crew of cheerleaders can be another help to you. This process you are embarking on can be difficult. Having some individuals who can give you genuine moral support and affirmation, and can rekindle your enthusiasm when it inevitably flags at periodic intervals, is another important component in your support team.

Also, you need a body of people who can provide information to you at key points. People with insights to certain careers or jobs as they emerge in your thinking. People who can introduce you to other people, other resources, potential employers or backers. It is important to build that expanded people-network that you can draw upon.

In addition to these very worldly resources, there is also the resource of your faith. Whatever your spiritual belief structure or religious affiliation may be, if you conduct your career planning consistent with your faith your chances of success grow immensely. In whatever form or language you perceive your beliefs, opening yourself to the intentions and influences of your God, the Universe, your Angels or Nature brings to you a major added dynamic to your quest. Our whole objective ——— to plan our careers within the greater framework of fulfilling our life's direction ——— is inherently consistent with seeking such a larger spiritual support influence.

Done honestly, this can be a powerful influence to bring into your direction-setting and decision-making. But you need to be forewarned: this influence may not turn out in exactly the manner you might presuppose. The specific for which you ask for help may not be the specific that is returned. It often will not be. As has been said, God's answer to our prayers is sometimes "no." The more narrowly and specifically you frame your request for help, the *less* likely you will get what you ask for. God or the Universe will more likely respond to you in what is seen as the best response for you, the most meaningful response for you, based upon what you are truly seeking --- i.e. not finding a job, but fulfilling your life. "Best" from that larger perspective may be far beyond what you have been able to see thus far.

So if you choose to ask for this spiritual influence to be brought into your search and your decision making (and I encourage you to do so), then be prepared for the potential range of responses that may be returned. Ask for *guidance in your quest*, not the fulfillment of a narrow career selection you may have made. God and the Universe will not be complicit in your moving down a disadvantageous path, and will thereby seek to close doors to you where it deems appropriate. But God and the Universe can be enormously effective at providing positive choices to you. Through this process, be sure to regularly spend some quiet time in your spiritual practice. Listen for the quiet messages, watch for the subtle signals, and pay attention when out-of-left-field remarkable coincidences show up unexpectedly in your life.

There are other things at work here.

Recommendation: Do not ask for help from your spiritual relationships if you are not prepared to act on that help. If you do ask, be prepared for some incredible new experiences to be presented to you.

14. PASSION

Be Careful of the Lit Match.

You may have noticed the absence to this point of any discussion in this writing about "career passion." Typical of most career planning books is the encouragement, if not the success measure, that you should feel passionate about the career you choose, passionate about the work you do. Such passion will ensure success and satisfaction with your career and your work.

If the career or job you select also happens to reflect an area in your life for which you feel great passion, that may be a right combination that will work successfully for you. But it is not a requirement. If you have determined that your job is a *separate* support tool to enable the larger priorities in your life, job passion may well be a negative force in your life structure, working against and distracting your ability to focus and achieve those primary goals.

Passion is another one of those many double-edged swords that continually present themselves to us in our lives. We need to be very cautious in our assessment of what that passion really represents to us, and how it plays into our life. Many times we equate passion with what is actually a personal compulsory drive; we elevate our work into a life mission that is well beyond what is needed; we seek to achieve, or push others to achieve, goals that are either unrealistic or inappropriate to the need or circumstance. We may fully believe and claim that our passion reflects the opportunity to do good great things for others, whereas in fact it represents an opportunity for us to achieve a personal success. In short, the passion we claim may simply be the cover story for our own ambitions, however nobly stated. The passion is not one of giving, it is one of consumption.

If you should get caught in this easy trap, you will have surrendered your life rather than fulfilled your life. You will have become a prisoner in yet another form to your job, whereas your goal was to position your job so that it *served* your life.

If passion plays a role here, then I would encourage you to be passionate about your life and its fulfillment. Be passionate about character, about ethics, about truth and honesty, about taking personal responsibility and keeping your word, about contributing to a good that is greater than yourself. Be passionate about curiosity, learning, and growing. Be passionate about people and what affects them. Be passionate about including in your life a respect and a practice for something larger than yourself and your immediate world. And then be forgiving to yourself when your passion occasionally falls short, when your passion clouds your best judgment, or when your passion leads you into territory in which you should best not go. Respect the limits of passion, and distinguish between that passion that serves as good fuel for your personal motivation versus that passion that is excess energy that is out of control and scattered. Temper your passion not with indifference, but with wisdom. Use your passion, but do not allow yourself to be used by it.

15. SOME CONCLUDING THOUGHTS ...

It's your Life. Live it.

Is your job important?

No, as far as whether you select one specific activity over another option. WHY you select that particular option is more important than WHAT you select. Whether your career choice allows you to fulfill your life's larger purposes — whether directly or indirectly ─── is the truly important decision criteria.

Yes, to the extent that it matches up well with fulfilling your life and making it possible for you to contribute what you have to the world, to accomplish the spiritual goals that are in front of you, and to realize the best essence of yourself and your gifts.

There are no rights or wrongs to labor under. No declaratory judgments to be made. No successes or failures, just turns in the road that teach you and guide you in your life's journey. Seek only to continually clarify your intentions, become clearer about what you are seeking to achieve beyond the daily workday, and to know more fully what is really meaningful in your life. Then find what will help make that truer you happen. And remember that today's decisions are not forever. They are merely the raw material that prepares you for the next wonderful phase of your life.

"I know of no more encouraging fact than the unquestioned ability of man to elevate his life by a conscious endeavor. It is something to be able to paint a particular picture, or to carve a statue, and so to make a few objects beautiful; but it is far more glorious to carve and paint the very atmosphere and medium through which we look, which morally we can do. To affect the quality of the day, that is the highest of arts. Every man is tasked to make his life, even in its details, worthy of the contemplation of his most elevated and critical hour."
—Henry David Thoreau

APPENDIX 1:

References and Footnotes

(1) ACT Institutional Data File, published in University Business, November 2006 issue.

> 2005 1st to 2nd Year Retention Percentages
> 2-year public institutions: 51.6%
> 2-year Private institutions: 61.7%
> 4-year public institutions: 66.4%
> 4-year Private institutions: 70.9%

(2) *Measuring Up 2006: The National Report Card on Higher Education*; The National Center for Public Policy and Higher Education

(3) Time Magazine study, Sources: U.S. Census Bureau; LandScan 2003/UT-Battelle, LLC

(4) Center for Retirement Research, Boston University

(5) 2005 *New Face of Work Survey*, MetLife Foundation/Civic Ventures

(6) Daniel Kadlec, TIME Magazine, September 25, 2006 issue.

(7) This story courtesy of HomeandHolidays.com web site

(8) AARP Magazine, November and December 2006, pg 98.

ABOUT THE AUTHOR

Randy Bell's spiritual path has taken him to many diverse sources, though he is principally a follower of the teachings of Jesus of Nazareth, Buddha, Lao-Tsu, and has been a Zen practitioner for 40 years. He lives in the mountains of western North Carolina where he is the Founder and Director of Spring Creek Spirituality. He has written twelve previous books, writes two blogs on a variety of spiritual and social commentary topics, serves as a guest speaker / session leader, and leads spiritual and personal growth workshops and retreat sessions. He is a member of North Carolina Writer's Network, and Spiritual Directors International.

www.RandyBellSpiritualTeacher.blogspot.com

www.SpringCreekSpirituality.com

OTHER PUBLICATIONS BY RANDY BELL

(Published at www.McKeeLearningFoundation.com)

Books:
God and Me: A Statement of Belief
    ISBN-13:   978-0-9710549-5-0

Lessons from the Teacher Jesus
    ISBN-13:   978-0-9710549-2-9

Lessons from the Teacher Buddha
    ISBN-13:   978-0-9710549-7-4

Lessons from the Teacher Muhammad
    ISBN-13:   978-0-9710549-9-8

Lessons from the Teacher Moses
    ISBN-13:   978-0-9710549-8-1

Buddhism: An Introductory Guide
    ISBN-13   978-0-9710549-1-2

Forms of Meditation
    ISBN-13:   978-0-9710549-6-7

Starting a Personal Meditation Practice
    ISBN-13:   978-0-9895428-0-7

Unpacking The Boxes of Our Attachments
    ISBN-13:   978-0-9895428-1-4

Awareness, Insight & Mindfulness: 3 Steps on the Path to Wisdom
    ISBN-13:   978-0-9895428-4-5

The Myths of Our Founding Fathers and Their Constitution
ISBN-13:   978-0-9895428-3-8

Executive's Guidebook for Institutional Change
ISBN-10:   0-9710549-0-8

Various other spiritual essays and reference documents.

<u>**Blog Commentaries**</u>:

Thoughts From The Mountain
www.ThoughtsFromTheMountain.blogspot.com
A social commentary from a spiritual and ethical perspective.

Our Spiritual Way
www.OurSpiritualWay.blogspot.com
sharing our spiritual journeys together.

<u>**Contact**</u>:

Info@McKeeLearningFoundation.com

Info@SpringCreekSpirituality.com

www.ingramcontent.com/pod-product-compliance
Lightning Source LLC
Chambersburg PA
CBHW022201080426
42734CB00006B/535